Alan Morrison

A Tapestry of Absent Sitters

First published in 2009
by Waterloo Press (Hove)
95 Wick Hall
Furze Hill
Hove BN3 1NG

Printed in Palatino 10.7pt by
One Digital
54 Hollingdean Road
East Sussex BN2 4AA

A CIP record for this book is available
from the British Library

ISBN 978-1-906742-04-1

Acknowledgements

Thanks to the editors of the following journals and webzines in which some of these poems have appeared: *Autumn Leaves, Cadenza, Candelabrum, The Cannon's Mouth, The Journal, The London Magazine, Poet-in-Residence, Poetry Monthly, Poetry Salzburg Review, Pulsar* and *The White Leaf Review.*

'Raging Grains' was featured in the anthology *Orphans of Albion* (Sixties/Survivors' Presses, 2008).

Thanks to the following persons for having helped me focus to bring my second volume to its fruition through a highly testing but grounding period in my life: *Sebastian Barker, Brian Beamish, Leon Brown, Norman Buller, Andy Croft, Jan Hill, John Horder, Simon Jenner, David Kessel, John O'Donoghue, Sally Richards, Kevin Saving, Pauline Suett-Barbieri, Barry Tebb, Gwilym Williams;* and my most grounding influence of all, *Matilda, my Viking Queen.*

By the same author

Giving Light (Waterloo Press, 2003)
Clocking-in for the Witching Hour (Sixties Press, 2004)
Feed a Cold, Starve a Fever (Sixties Press, 2004)
The Mansion Gardens (Paula Brown, 2006)
Picaresque (chipmunkapublishing, 2008)

Other appearances

Don't Think of Tigers (The Do Not Press, 2001)
O the Windows of the Bookshop Must Be Broken – David Kessel
Collected Poems (editor & prefacer; Survivors' Press, 2005)
Orphans of Albion (Sixties/Survivors' Press, 2008)
The Night Shift (Five Leaves Publications, 2009)

Contents

III: *A Pageant of Abstracts*

IV: *Tracing the Pattern*

V: *A Tapestry of Absent Sitters*

For my mother, Helen

LONG time a child, and still a child, when years
Had painted manhood on my cheek, was I, —
For yet I lived like one not born to die;...
...Nor child, nor man,
Nor youth, nor sage, I find my head is gray,
For I have lost the race I never ran

Hartley Coleridge

I

Agitpropos

Praise with Faint Damnation
for Kevin Saving

Don't damn with faint praise or admiration –
Drub our green words till they bruise at the smart.
Raze us to grain, praise with faint damnation.

Feel free to deflate with defamation –
Pick at the scraps of the amateur heart,
Don't damn with faint praise or admiration.

Anything but vague, blanched affirmation –
Rattle our talents with your crafty art,
Raze us to grain, praise with faint damnation.

We're not after plaudits or salvation,
Blast against the grain that splits us apart –
Don't damn with faint praise or admiration.

Trample us to our naïf foundation,
We'll grasp the straws at the pitch of your dart;
Raze us to grain, praise with faint damnation.

No time for hyperbole's temptation:
We'd sooner upset Fashion's applecart –
Don't damn with faint praise or admiration;
Raze us to grain, praise with faint damnation.

The Clattering Classes

Discarded on the curling pavement slabs
crouched the beetly dark grey UNDERWOOD,
shining levers stirruped in,
compacted as a swatted fly;
long-hammered keys, fingertip-blunted,
an eroded causeway of QWERTYU.

I claimed the decrepit old typewriter,
cradled it in my arms, careful
not to let it fall and shatter
as if it were my own dust-cocooned soul,
a little broken but still dormant;
reflexive; reactive against the bland
craven anvil of a hammering scene
crimped in brinkmanship, besotted by
sameness, an understated take
on what has to be said, by not saying it.

Suggestion needs a kick-start now and then
or it whimpers out to nothing. Roaring voices,
hardly audible for stacking attacks
on life-quarried lines; belletrist backlash
against fired minds' spined generations;
an anti-crusade for the sake of staking
vain claims on the creaming page,
buttered self-tributes, owing nothing
to a Blasting past. The Thatcherwrite hack.

They have it all wrapped up now;
creativity need no more question.
*We know this, we know this – but never show
we know, too obvious. Show don't tell.*
Deconstructing the poets, stripping their spell.

Elocution Lessons

They sussed I scrubbed up from humble origins
by how my second-hand clothes wore me out
of pocket, kept up stay-press pretensions
of 'well-heeled'; my clipped articulation –
practically accentless – betraying embarrassment
at state-school culling: too conscious of aitches
to pass for one above my fricative station.

Those old-tie school boys deloused my foibles
as psychiatrists their patients' phobias,
with lackadaisical lazy-lashed flicks –
You lack that certain air... didn't rattle me,
salted as I was with socialist distaste
for privilege-peppered classes. Though I
resented those tongues ironing out my creases.

Naturally snatches of taut consonants
and cavalier vowels rubbed off on my palette
but not that lofty atmosphere
orbiting moon-cool composure;
gravity-defying, gravitas-supplying,
tripping high to satellites of expectation.

Fantasia on a Theme by Thomas Hardy

Never have ideas above your station,
      it'll only end poorly;
Remember that cloister-struck stonemason,
      darkling Jude Fawley.

A greengage when he spied those skerries
      of sandstone, and they spires
Sparking his eyes as blackest blackberries
      unreachable on the greenbriers.

Those spires he saw were Devil's horns
      leading him astray
From knowing's roses to knowledge's thorns
      that strip the heart away.

Time fleeced Jude's future – his wool eyes
      unravelled from their books:
Lambs snagged on barbs by hushaby
      box-cords tied to hooks.

He died in thrall of his tall vamps
      to peals of Trinity –
But tolling cow-bells, tumbril champs
      chimed his varsity.

In their flowing gowns those dons n' deans
      they rascal jackdaws be:
Cawing in ruins cut out of dreams
      of low-born boys as 'e.

The ink that stains their lily white
      dainties b'ain't the dirt
That fills your fingernails a'night
      n' soils your patched-up shirt.

The only verse you'll plough verbatim
        is the stump-jumped furrow there –
That plank for kneading bitumen:
        the only mortar-board you'll wear.

Those tasselled hats graduands throw
        to their Christminster sky:
Good as a cloud of cackling crows
        to the scarecrow's half-cocked eye.

Stones & Mortar-Boards

Intellect is catechised
Through tradition's tutelage;
Disciplined by licking cords,
Choristered on pristine sheets.

Blazered ranks are classicised
And classed in private cribbage –
Straw-boatered, tread the springboards
Tripping footlight to staged feats.

No surprise those scrolls are prized,
Prestige-steeped in steepled Oxbridge –
Streams of downcast mortar-boards
Millipede the chiselled streets.

Those differently exercised
Towards the greater suffrage
Take the bench, or misericords
Of Parliament's selective seats.

Obscure scholars have disguised
As steeplejacks, scaffold-cortege
Of stonemasons' processions scored
By chisels' contrapuntal beats.

No surprise those scrolls are prised,
Prestige-steeped in steepled Oxbridge –
Millipedes of mortar-boards
Stream the chiselled streets.

Ambitions cracked as Latinised
Spines in peeling linage
Of Herodotus, over-pored –
Doomed as fox-prowled bleats.

The un-shepherded and ill-advised
In under-funded umbrage,
Cast sights and floater votes towards
Democracies' disguised elites.

No surprise those scrolls are prized,
In dream-spiring Oxbridge –
Gowned jackdaws in mortar-boards
Millipede the chiselled streets.

A Stone's Throw

There goes Polyphemus,
Kerb-bound troglodyte.
He's got his one red eye on you
And on his Diamond White.

Here comes limping Oedipus
Dragging his swollen leg;
Guinea-pig of self-injecting,
Needle for a peg.

There's Medusa furnishing
Her flattened card-box home.
Every nickel chucked at her
Turns into a stone.

Rainbow Road

Routine is a beast to be slain – Vachel Lindsay

1. *Burnt Orange*

Day unpeels.
The defunct department store drapes laundry
of burnt orange SALE signs out to dry.
Last flags of trade before scaffolding
abseils up to refurbish Co-Op
kitsch with IKEA-kitted flats –
ONLY THREE DAYS LEFT reflects
a brutal eschatology.
    From carved Scandinavian chic
to oaky dark Slovakian café,
cave for singed light-sensitives
killing their cravings with slaking lattes,
cracked cadavers gnarled coarsely as
roughshod grooves on the chestnut counter.

2. *Khaki Green*

This thrift-road flares occasionally
with black and sea-green rainbows
on radical Saturdays.
Protestors parade second-hand placards
of lobotomised monkeys
to 'WHEN DO WE WANT IT?' – *NOW*
uncompromisingly grubby, captured
by the rustic crackle of *The Cowley Club*'s
flaking khaki, sanctuary for
spliffing fringes, wormwood door
emphatically latched like an anarchist tract –
wood-rimmed display of agitprop throwing
pamphlet-thin shouts at ear-phoned browsers
mobbed by mimes of muted porchway-sitters,
day-evicted tenants of the YMCA's
epic peeling pilasters.

3. *Deep Red*

Hope holds out at the squatters' pitch
abrading the land grab by
reclaiming lath and plaster empties:
the deserted cream and red Methodist hall
now sloganeers GOD HATES YOU THAT'S WHY
HE'S LETTING YOU DIE – STOP CORPORATE
SELL OFFS, Diggers with whorled dreadlocks
uphold the tracts of Winstanley,
and I, an unsocial socialist,
thank God for their ragged crop.

4. *Seagull Grey*

Cash-confirmands consult their souls'
overdrafts, genuflect to
chrome gods, hoping to gain Salvation
at 0% APR –
sins' atoning pins tapped in,
plastic transubstantiates
into tonguing notes; unleavened paper,
franked with false idols. Sudden rush
of endorphins: any purchase appears
possible from tilted views
afforded by giants' shoulders.

Rental potential shored in the moulded
shop-tops' seagull-shit grey.

5. *Acid Yellow*

Each day, the nicotine-stained same,
acid yellow as a stamp-licker's tongue:
Eternal Return at first hand
in daily routine, strait-jacketing
the spirit's intensity. Scraping
coppers only deemed tender when

dished out by cloudy shop-keepers,
but seldom exchanged by postal workers
of sub-contracted consciences:
sorting-office Protestants.

Trapped in rented versions of life;
crippled by credit; ambered in arrears;
bowed to standing orders; pinned-down
by debits. No traceable point to determine
the rights of life's short-hold. Small print:
a Braille that bribes our lives, along
with the Bank's pulped peppermint.

Nights scrape perfection. The asthmatic tap
splutters on the basin's flannel tramp.

6. *Cheapside Blue*

From sophomoric morning
wrecking-balls holler gun-shots
dismantling the bric-a-brac
of this rainbow-terraced town.
Carcinogens prove schismatic:
smoking bans abound while cars
are sacrosanct as the middle class.
Carbon claws our way to the stars.

Sirens remix the curfew chimes.
By the Council Board divided:
fly-tipping circuses of flea routines.
A nation of tenants and landlords
and sofa-surfers on ironing-boards.
Astute graffiti states: *Burning Times.*

Who's to give the nostalgia-tagged
paraphernalia shops a quote?
Not the pencilled cheapside sky
smudging like a suicide note
in the dripping awning of the eye.

Three Street Scenes

i. The Metaphor on the Pavement

There he exists on the pavement side
the knotted metaphor, worsted in a clump
of ripped and stained rags, soiled and piss-smelling,
yellow tongue flashing 'spare any change?'

This ground-welded metaphor is an entire thing,
owns nothing, needs nothing but sustenance, a bite
to get him through another street-betrayed moment;
all he has is carried on his back, in his pockets,
is inside his shell, visible to all
in tortuous detail: sun-burnished skin,
stubble, odour, tattooed forearms, ear ring –
he is there, before us, existence distilled,
freed from the trappings of material things
into Hellish enlightenments: no need for
un-thirst-quenching objects, inedible
possessions, all hollow as his plunging gut –
so what use are those coins we chuck at him,
except to shed from our own shells
tender that strips us of ourselves?

The metaphor throws back
many copper eyes at us.

ii. His Eyes, Evicted

A clotted youth has his greasy head down
on a step for a hard-worn pillow
outside the stucco Lodge, where, nearby,
keeping out of the sun, a secrecy of Masons
crouch in sweating suits, smoking.

An obsolete proprietor, cardiganed incarnadine,
lapses back into the tattered shadows of his stamp shop
that hasn't seen sunlight in the last dragged years.

The youth lifts up his face, skin scuffed and wrinkled
before its time, bruised by bad luck's knuckles –
young-in-kind, but less unlived-in than many his age;
a gutted squatter's scarpered digs; his eyes,
evicted, try to keep their shattered glass intact,
taped-up with patches, plasters, grubby bandages;
the puffing wolf blows his fag-paper life
into each stripped day, crutched on discarded cigs.

iii. The Pavement Piper

Back against marble cold,
Sat on card,
The Pavement Piper plays;
A Tunnel Bard.

A passer by drops a coin
Into a cap
Then sits upon a bench
Paper in lap.

All the Piper has to sell
Is his pipe's song
But tunes cannot be bought
By anyone.

The Strawberry Thieves

A man should put his heart into his work, and that work should be
the kind that he can care about   – William Morris

They filch my crust, lay waste my dreams,
But I'd not disturb them in their pursuit
Of robbing me of my only means
To bear any edible fruit,
Because the sight is beautiful as wallpaper

Blooming with flowers. Scamped in haste.
Creased over vaster walls of betters.
There to peel from porridgy paste
Steadily as grafting debtors'
Balsam-stripped hands. Time's itchy draper

Doesn't darn what it tears, just stitches
And glues the splitting seams;
Too busy counting its riches
To notice the fabric of dreams
Tangibly swirling, sprawling on paper.

Lowest of the low, I, decorator,
Pasting-up patterns from a blue-handed man
Of vision on blind walls. I, dumb curator,
Smoothing high sights with spattered tan
On vein-raised hands that crawl and taper.

There blushes the *Strawberry Thief*:
Brown-spotted thrushes on indigo set
Nestled in pouting calico leaf
Pilfering strawberries weals of my sweat
Ripen to gross for the gaffers' wage-caper.

But I can't begrudge them in doing so well:
They scoff the profits from the fruits of my labour:
They own the punnets my strawberries swell.

Thought Hobos

The man with the forceful opinions
Is infinitely malleable:
Bigotry more often beguiles behind
The beam of an amiable liberal.
The radical's prone to bi-polar swings,
From extremes to bourbon creams,
But always arrives back at the middle
By the time he's beaten his means.
The long-in-the-tooth hypocrite
Is a self-pillorying sample:
He condemns other people for profiting
From his prickly example.
When push comes to shove, only the lunatic
Can be certain of anything scientific.

The Right-Hand Side of the Brain
for David Kessel

Art is the product of society, as the pearl is the product of the oyster,
and to stand outside art is to stand inside society –
                    Christopher Caudwell, *Illusion and Reality*

In oak-panelled Toynbee Hall, crouched historically
in Aldgate's maze of bitten bricks – dirt-orange
as flossed sweets foraged under tatty settees –
huddles of fossilised Communists
commemorate Caudwell's cloud-realities
and lucid illusions. Thought might be matter.
What else are these red faces thronging here
but moving, speaking, gesturing thoughts?
(Shuddering prospect: some of my thoughts
are violent; destructive). Time for re-constructive!
Revolution looks possible in the simmering streets.
A coup de tat of thoughts riots in our heads.

The fire alarm punctuates the speakers' polemic –
MI5…? posits one conspiracy conscript;
(*Or MFI?*, quip I).   How to reach the means
in parameters of tongues? Truth bashes taste-buds
to numbness. We live in dialectics –
see the tramped man bowling cracked hands outside
the restaurant blistering over the street.
Blind peace in blasted times. Conscience shrinks
in the shadows of creaking BUY TO LET signs.

In hall, we scrappy few cough to the choir
of the Strawberry Thieves, churning our morale;
a flock of dowdy jackdaws in the ruins of our ism,
pack up our wings and croak *The Internationale…*

…but in this ideological desert
we might as well be legionnaires
pimped into sun-bashed képi blancs
sands gulping our camel tracks,
and instead be mumbling *Le Boudin…*

The Patient Blaze
for Andy Croft

Splinters thorn the mangy lion's paw –
Once vigorous as granite, atlas-planted,
Conviction's innate light, the atheist's faith,
Invincible vision of saintlier times,
Aslan ablaze, roaring mane, prideful strut
Leading by pamphlet example, lighting minds
In spite of oppositions' dark pragmatics
Screening stuffed Darwinian cynicism:
Man is a mammal, a Mammon, a manimal.

Why now the jungle liberator groaning
In binds, its bald paws molting alopecia
Lifeless as snow, splayed, rag-tagged, yet
Lingering silently, an autistic stray

Shambling aimlessly from distance to distance?
Unfinished binds buckle its barbed spine with
Rickets of trapped potential, untapped.
Vigilantes bait it, brand its dowdy coat
Indelibly with *scorched philosophy* – but
Victory would kill it: only inner-fire can raze
Empires, through failure's slow-burning blaze.

Country of Ghosts

This mongrel island long ago
sought to control the ebb and flow
of its spiritual populace –
conducted a supernatural census
on those haunts that cast some doubt
on the patriotic devout
among our antecedents,
troubling their bowed descendants.
Lingering spirits of idealists
and un-translated socialists –
Winstanley, Lilburne, Robert Owen,
Keir Hardie, Robert Smillie, Bevan,
Robin Hood – all shown the door
in spite of claims to common folklore
and homegrown convictions.
These draconian evictions
raised the odd liberal eyebrow, but the
ever-accommodating C of E
toned down the Rituale Romanum
to lighter terms – how modern of them.

Dreamers and altruists vanished
from public plinths, banished
any traces of their sway.
(Naturally Oliver Cromwell could stay
planted in front of Parliament
for he was pro-establishment
bar one regicidal lapse.)
But these measures were perhaps
unnecessary since word spread
of exodus of the left-wing dead.
The worst offenders, apparently,
had long opted for purgatory
over damp haunts where they were ignored
in our mossbacked Kingdom; or posts abroad.

But a new threat stalks the mortal Brits
from potent continental culprits:
scores of European souls
now championing the spirit-proles –
rumour has it Marx, Sartre, Trotsky,
Saint-Simon, Vaillant, Lafarge, Gorky,
number among them – are bent on
transmigrating to our nation.
So, before they reach our shores
our leaders shut the Dover doors,
tighten up the protocols:
border, book, candle controls.

The Declarers

You're hounded, hunted at every turn;
bound in labours barring abilities,
eroding chores called 'jobs',
abrading potential untapped
till your brow's as chafed as cuttlefish.
Your labour, quarried for others' profits.
Scraping cramped solace from two stitched days
a week, punctuated callously by
the flogging clock's ticking ultimatums:
spare time is limited, spare time limited –
whittled down fast to the utilitarian
varicose tallow.
              Time to time, you're burnt
by un-abating binds; bow out on chits,
prescriptive plasters, pressurised to
return to work before the singe has healed.
Hounded, hunted, month in, month out,
veiled threats seeding the GP's lips.
Take the middle path, try balancing
stress and pressing necessity,
build on opportunities to tug you out
of the giro-or-biro trap – paltry tot
of top-up to unbefitting benefits.

No such witch hunts for white City collars
whose undeclared winnings and bogus bonuses
go unnoticed by taxmen and ministers –
and when the mighty fall off their betting hedges
for speculating, the taxed and the scrapped
are clapped in stocks to bail their gambling out.

Meantime Satanic ads hector claimants
into coming clean, so losing out more:
therapeutic earnings pooled into shortfalls
of 'pinch-some' support – tripped up by pitfalls.
Barred dole-eyes, heed the baleful BEWARE,
spared to private poverty, as long as you declare.

The Recusants (1586 – 1986)

Our natures, frayed with sun-warped books
blanched khaki in the window beam;
cobwebbed in spider-hatching nooks
behind the hulking curtain screen
thick as the gown on plaster Mary
enshrined in the spare unpainted room.

Hood-souls, crouched in contrary
cottage-dark where doubts mushroom,
plunge the nicotined reredos
into outer blackness. — Biding
by altar-jambs, we ghost a cross
in the rigged ballot – then into hiding
opinions in empty larder priest-holes,
cowed by the blue torch Goosy-Gander.

Too strapped for brass, too bookish for proles,
our emblem, a grounded germander;
recusants of class – rubbed rosaries
for worry beads; drubbed socialism
waxing in candle-lit crannies.

Scrapers of coupon catechism
trampled by the Thatcher anathema –
snagged grants bar university
for familial fiscal asthma:
lapsed capitalists in bankruptcy.

Our stomachs howl hosts of weak refills
from stewed tea-bags: we fast past Lent.
Episcopacies of toast-racked bills
numb us to TV's otiose vent,
while our own obscure, un-broadcast soap
is watched by the set-top's porcelain Pope.

The Plaster Tramp
for Sebastian Barker

Gloomy morning, stewed from dreams
to an unclouded voice downstairs
drifting up through the ceiling beams
with a hint of incense, half-answered prayers.

I find my parents beatified on
respite from debt through alms; the fume
beading their heaped faces, briefly gone.
An aura of calm haloing the room.

Fear temporarily slopes into hope
as the plaster tramp seems to wink and grin
magically from its mantelpiece cope,
immortalised in glossed chagrin.

Through smudging years, that plaster tramp
caricatured our stony lot;
crinkled into bilious life like the damp
trumpeting the walls with rot.

The carrageen of repossession
stalked a clan of craned Canutes –
bracing wills at seas of recession –
neck-bent and pear-shaped as lutes.

Transplanted from that plaster tramp,
my adumbrated vagrant future:
captured bench-napping in the cramp
of a sculptor's time-trapped suture.

Indebted to days of alms and no phone,
insights of stripped-down poverty:
the tattered chair, no quixotic throne
had our house mushroomed commodity.

All material things appeared transparent
as the luminous fuse in me that frayed
my stripling grasp of tangible apparent;
toys turned to tomb relics, painted to fade

after my time.
                    — Not the inanimate
tramp that matters in that plaster-past,
just the aura that haloed its insensate
sentiment; what the eye can't cast.

The Crack on the Vase

for James
To be is to be perceived – George Berkeley

'It's symbolic' murmured James,
my unknowingly Thomistic brother,
at the hairline crack crawled suddenly
on the dusty vase of poverty's salvage.
A sudden charge shone out from it
(not solely of it, projected *into* it
by our aesthetic artifice –
a reciprocal echo). It had
become something other
than a vase, now brimming
with sentiments in our animating
gaze. In a moment's enchantment we'd
cast an animistic spell, oblivious ourselves
to power ebbing from us – an outer *ents vital* (or
humming electricity) – now beaming something into
us we weren't aware of; a new-perceived significance;
haecceity. No more observers, now observed, as when hid in
the shadier pews to avoid serving on the altar, but still visible
to the priest's hunched helper, her vision all-observing as God's
(two genuflected trees pretending absence in empty quads);
haloed by holiness in objects obscured by style's crudity;
obfuscated by the surface (the material always nauseated
us, in spite of our catholic taste); the sudden emitting
shine on the vase ovaling our reflective faces. Was
that the collective soul we glimpsed in the
vase's vague glimmer? Connaturality
of all things we sensed, called it
compassion, socialism, this
airy quiddity, soul politic,
spiritual polish – but
it had no name, no
verbal tarnish, that
was its natural
poetry. All we knew
was the vase, ourselves, our
souls — none of them belonged to us.

Sprig of the Broom

Michael (Edward Lord) Abney Hastings,
reluctant Plantagenet Heir Apparent

Apparently the last Plantagenet
capers obscurely down under,
indifferent as corks on a swagman's hat
to the outback's ancestral thunder.
Whence came his name? From an ancestor,
Matilda-waltzing Geoff of Anjou
whose branches snagged on *planta genista:*
his tag for donning the sprig of a broom.

Adopted by York to blazon his yolk
from Curtmantle, a superior claim
to the throne usurped by Bollingbroke
to accidental Lancastrian reign
through habit-forming throne-sitting
past incapacitated kith –
a thorn in the side of his prickly King,
neurasthenic Henry the Sixth,

sparking dynastic war (long-reckoned:
the branches had been rocking with tension
since the uncrowning of Richard the Second,
unable to tell his own reflection –
even in the mirror of his father-in-law,
fragile Charles the Sixth of France,
who had to be treated delicately or
he'd shatter into splinters of glass).

York was slain but the white rose bloomed
back into power through his son Edward
and in turn *his* sons, princes groomed
but nipped in the bud by Uncle Richard
(the Third), the last Plantagenet King:
a Pretender dismounted Crookback's reign
in a hacking glade. A disgraced sibling,
Clarence, transplanted abroad with the name.

Is it a genetic memory blade
jarred on the stabbing of Crookback
that the last Plantagenet prefers the shade
of a coolibah in the outback?
Crookback's crown snagged on a barb
of a broom, there plucked and donned
by an obscure dynastic valley arb
from the borders of bloodlines beyond.

And it's been borrowed since, for seven-
hundred odd years: through dour Tudors,
peruked Stuarts, rouged Georges, Wettins
of Saxe-Coburg-Gotha (Windsors)...
Monarchists might want to further take note
of a genealogical quandary,
when waving their Jacks at the Royal float:
of the alleged illegitimacy

of Edward the Fourth – the vital sliver
of blood-line between old and new:
that in the broom's absence a bowman's quiver
usurped the purple with Baylbourne blue.
If so, by primogeniture's lay,
Clarence's scion is – to use the Aus lingo –
our King *dinkum*: a Republican, blasé
as the bat, the kanga and leveller dingo.

[Notes: Baylbourne is the surname of the archer whom some revisionist historians allege may have been the real father of Edward Plantagenet, later Edward IV. If true, this would have made Clarence aka George Plantagenet, by the law of primogeniture, the legitimate heir to the throne. Michael Abney Hastings is apparently a direct descendant of Clarence. 'the bat, the kanga and leveller dingo' is a parody of the anti-Plantagenet rhyme 'the cat, the rat and Lovell our dog/ Rule all England under the hog', by William Collingbourne].

Organ Grind

Thirteen years in a wilderness of faithlessness and fear
churn my stewed emotions with a dry religious tear.
Inside a something stirs – is it my recusant soul?
For missing time the spirit's slept; faith's been on the dole.
An absent-minded spire tempts me in to the quiet retreat
of a church's tomb-cool shade out from the sweating street:
pagan pant of heated tongues, carnality of bars,
bestialities of shops, sun-bleached bursting bras...
I once served on a similar altar to the one I stare at now.
With rising sense of reverence I genuflect and bow
before the picture-cloth of Christ. Hide behind a pew.
Cross myself with instinct twice as doubting Catholics do.
I pant a prayer, then panic at the piercing reredos.
Hoist my flagstone-scraping eyes up to the yard-arm Cross.
Gaze above to architraves – St. Peter's vaulted roof:
stained-glass paned depictions of the Passion without the proof.
Sudden as a mood descends, an incense in the mind,
vast flue-pipes vibrate to swell the thundering organ grind.
Bellows wheeze and shudder; spine timbres into boon,
rising to the chord cascade of the stripped cathedral tune.
Spirits stride in vertigos of vaults as wind-grooves pound.
Something stirs inside me, amplifies me off the ground;
my hairs prick up as if by spider legs in scaling wind –
is it a spiritual or primal thing that shivers to this grind?

Shrewsbury Apercu
for Leon Brown

...on flagstones of the market square
a ranter's quaking tracts instruct
the thunder, lightning rhetorical;
ancient, rustic, puritanical
as sandstone; time-stained architecture,
dusted, chiselled, hypocritical.
A masonry-armoured knight on watch.
A chain-mailed dog in the porticoed
alcove above Angevine shields
under the recalcitrant clock...

Portly horsehaired Indian Clive,
obese in bronze, planted astride
imperial plinth in posthumous heat
with Galapagos-Beagling Darwin,
lugubrious mutton-chopped Orangutan
chomping theories through the leaves
outside his russet house a stone's throw
down the cramping links of crooked
Tudor shop-tops jutting timbered
mandibles into the street –
latticed and latched to a battened time.
Portals of shuffling metallic machines
gift paper Darwins stripped from trees
that crackle in grasping hands.

Troglodyte gazes traipse boutiques.
Cro Magnon sons and grabbers
of greed-leashed, mortgaged generations,
are lambasted by the bible-
thumper from the Marches
(*homo evangelicus*)
stalking mocha-lapping sceptics
perched on benches like prehensile
jackdaws in Trappist ruins;
pavement-scraping breed;

.

kinks in creation's crinkled spine
split by ice and chancels.
Churches, colossal-planted dinosaurs
fossilised to curiosities
housing long-swallowed sarcophagi
stone-weighted in time's dark bowels;
mausoleums of clamshell infinities...

This parochial nook, Lilliputian-mapped,
a time-brined Middlemarch horse-George
immortalised; cog-stopped tomb
of ghosted industry, unvisited...
little-pillared labyrinth of iced-almond houses,
slumbering churchyards and cobbled winds...

I picture Lydgate, ideals as high
as his stovepipe, unstitching polite
society with scalpelling eye,
pinning ideals like butterflies –
his disappointment at one old peer
throwing in the shovel of his Digger dream
in the woods, for a more grounded career.

Tree-tumbled, twittering antecedents
grappled from trees to quarried plinths –
keep getting taller, arms bowing longer,
galumphing into visceral futures.
Ancient branches rock more and more
appealingly – Darwin's cul-de-sac:
some seem ripe to re-uptake
their swaying ancestral seats.
                              Should we
be punished for anthropomorphic lapse?
Chased out from houses to scourge of small cords,
dragged out from the apse
bowed down on all fours
on flagstones of the market square...

Absolute Berliners

i. *Neuköln*

An English neurotic in Neuköln,
sore eyes soothed by painterly daubs
of pink cherry blossoms softening
Prussian grey terraces stiff as sentries
on the straight unbending will of the street,
interspersed with peach and pale orange
from subtler Ottoman palettes.

Berlin, self-denying; allied bombs
realigned you, cauterised your classicism,
like the fall, rise and decline of the
Holocaust Memorial's sable causeway
of ebony slabs. *That's where the Hitler youth
held their first rally* jabs the loud hailer
of the burly German tour guide
at an unassuming sun-blanched platz.

ii. *The Wall*

The Wall: links of pocked concrete mural,
graffiti, scrawls, grotesques, statements
needing no translation, a tidal
wave of thronging faces spilling through
the parting bricks; a Curriculum
Vitae omitting all but dates –
spread on this canvas to Teutonic guilt...
...the East Side, still dismantling;
a Meccano hinterland; a mumbling
primordial suburbia limbering
on hind legs of dinosauric cranes –
West vestiges still tipping in,
sprawling billboards touting kitsch
pop icons beaming searchlight teeth
on the crumbled post-Communist bloc.

iii. *Alexanderplatz*

Marienkirche's weathervane
once compassed the highest view, now a
crouched casket of replicas and relics:
a Totentanz mosaic, baptismal
font wrapped with black dragons, two
melted bells – a third outside:
glowering Luther embattled in bronze,
gulped up by the craving shadow
of the cloud-pinioned Fernsehturm
spearing selective Heavens above
vast pavements of Alexanderplatz;
pewter Neptune and jade Dryads
fountain its centre with gushes of hands.

iv. *Brandenburg Gate*

Brandenburg Gate: Doric columns
prop a vast stacked mantle, ground
to the galloping Quadriga: winged
Viktoria steering her chariot of four
turquoise horses stilled in charge,
holding aloft an eagle-tipped staff
cruciformed with tarnished brand.

v. *The Reichstag*

The Reichstag's stark face stares abashed
like a half-forgiven ancestor,
its pillared mouth yawning a trail
of steps flat-lit as platitudes,
haunted still by nightmare-footage
of fudge-brown tunics, sharply cut
Hugo Boss black uniforms
ascending Aryan infamy –
but Berlin won't be blighted by
detritus of long-stripped histories,
defies one fissure in pantheist past

with splinter-bitten liberties
casting light no Titan shadows
of Fuhrer, Kaiser, Bismarck can dark.

vi. *Galleries of the Dead*

The silences between the headstones
in the writers' cemetery
lengthen with the scrolling shadows;
arcades of painted mortuaries;
freshly dug graves groaning humps
of cocoa-coloured loam: molehills
marking spots where poets and
philosophers have gone to earth,
or had their works newly exhumed.
Posterity mingles with fresh fumes
of coffee-ghosted galleries:
daubs of browns, greys, pale blues
in inked outlines by posthumous
Paula Modersohn, an almond-eyed
nocturnal kobold caught by night.

vii. *An Absolute Berliner*

A gypsy lady kneads a dowdy
gap-toothed accordion,
grins in the beating sun bearing
her yellowed ivories, adjusting
a polka dotted head scarf, flattered
I camera-frame her face carved out
of walnut-shell: her tawny skin
countenances all of time's
page-gnarled mistakes. Her bright
miraculous smile forgives my gaze
its rarely travelled greenness. She
busks in the dust of indifferent traffic,
moulding back into slow brown burn,
beaming, beaten, hopeful, vibrant
            as her absolute Berlin.

II

Swedish Suite

Tall Thoughts in Gamla Stan
for Matilda

Många bäckar små gör en stor å/ Many small brooks will form a river
                                                    – Swedish saying
From my graspless hand/ Drop friendship's precious pearls – Coleridge

Shadows stand tall in the Swedish light.
Lashes blink unaccustomed to
Gamla Stan's autumn stamina:
acrylic haven after England's watercolour.
Solar spots on the ocular halo,
retinas dazzled to sundogs arced
over Stockholm's huddled mushroom-patch
in Vädersolstavlan.
Takes time for clouds to acclimatise
as Sixteenth Century converts to
King Gustav Vasa's vision.
Scandinavian suaveness amazes
in stark light tricks of dark and day.
The silhouetted cityscape
prickly with contradicting spires,
inking alternative views.

Near Norrköping, a pavilion
stands haloed in gold and copper leaves.
Cathedrals of heady chardonnay light
pour royally down on a yellow and white
icing and marzipan palace.
Looming above, pillars of trees
impaled with bark-nailed Swedish Kings
flood Golgotha shadows on
the sloping cloudberry ground.

In the chilled haze of Lotorp's pines
ice-mists comb the forest floor,
web the trees in aspic of dewfall.
We forage for scatterings of chantarelles
careful not to tramp them to
squashed trumpets on the greasy leaves,
boot-trolling toadstool villages.

The moment's all we have breathes Berit
in sanguine owlish gasps
as she pours coffee from a flask,
coffee dark as the day is short
(says Matilda); I basket these
chance aphorisms in creaking wicker
as the Chanterelles compare themselves,
yellow-trunked and charcoal-roofed,
to sentry-boxes on Stadsholmen.

O to bribe Kronos with a krona.
But mortality gifts me Matilda
and light that accidents, distracts
time's fractured stare, transcendental
thought-patterns graspless as air.

Lakes sit piercing quiet, elliptic –
no birdsong, no tree-creak, no sound –
perhaps this is Valhalla?
Longship clouds row splashless oars
across the lake-reflected sky…

Long thoughts stand demure as stones
or introspective trolls…

                              …tall in the Swedish light.

[*Vädersolstavlan* 'The Sundog Painting' painted on the morning of
April 20th 1535 depicted sundogs (small incomplete rainbows) over
Stockholm – some at the time thought this meteorological phenomena
to be a sign that God was displeased with the then King Gustav's
conversion to Protestantism. *Stadsholmen* an island in Stockholm on
which the Royal Palace stands; it means, literally, *Island of the City*].

Seeing The Night Entirely

i.

On the train from Norrköping to Stockholm
I trundle from Sweden's unadulterated sun
back to England's vaguer skies
and watery countryside. As I
leave this sprawling, laky kingdom
I'm already returning, struck sights snagging
on pines, spires, standing stones poised in
smooth postures amid a wood-carved carriage,
carpentered to share while travelling.
An absence of classed compartments; a view
afforded everyone, not just a kept few.

Sweden is shared: you see this in its vast
rambling green, un-hedged, unfenced – perhaps
how England once was before the land grab
chequered it – sprawling boundlessly, verged
only by polite interruptions of trees,
pine forests sprung in orderly numbers
knowing the pastures need space to breathe
and gather their luminous green.

ii.

Norrköping, no in-grown provincial town,
but blossoming post-industrial
with flowering warehouses, trickling wharfs,
paper mills, factories transformed
into old-world curiosities:
the custard-yellow Museum of Labour,
shaped like a steam iron, stands miraculous
on a canal; a tall brick chimney
sprouts from the calm waters; nearby
a man-made falls rustles its applause.

A stone-grey building mumbling a sign
Rättvisa Solidaritet Socialism
levels the eye on a pavement corner,
a provincial feature – polls apart
from every drawn-curtained English town's
backstreet-crouched Conservative Club:
Sweden has ever held the evener view,
politics and skies of a very different blue.

iii.

I've come to see through the neighbourly
ease of fey Sweden – its yellow, blue, green
and russet wood hobbit-houses, white-decked
verandas; friendlier, less forbidding forests
soft-carpeted in moss; its wakeful nature's
summer insomnia, burring crickets
in the salmon-pink twilight of small
enchanted hours – that in vaguer England,
our clouded eyes have invented night:
a soupy stupor rinsed of ancient
magic, fairies, trolls, elves – conjured
still in Sweden's shadow-dappled woods
where elks' antlers crack like moving
branches through the brindled trees;
our own folkloric roots ploughed to
cloddish logic and chronic clocks...

in Sweden, this summer, there was no starless
darkness, I saw the night entirely in
pinks, whites, violets, and now I wonder
if dark is just another form of light
our eyes haven't yet adjusted to...

The Dead Falls
i.m. of Magnus Huss

A vast rupture splintering out to sea, the old lake
Ragunda blasted out by Magnus 'Wild' Huss,
accidental dam-builder, intending to bypass
the timber-crushing Rapids, emptying the lake
instead. Shareholders were compensated.
Waterless villagers' wraths, incurred.
Raged, they arranged another accident
this time involving Huss in a boat (enough said).
Later, they called this gaping cavity
The Dead Falls, a last sarcastic accolade
for their posthumous quarry's invisible rapids.
To capitalise on failure is the greatest form
of genius, and hapless Huss the barren
valley-maker almost pulled it off.
He'd achieved a lasting tribute to his blunder:
this great gorge of boulders, a billiard-balled ravine,
as if a rock troll had spat out its gnarled teeth,
or a spillage of age-dusted calcified droppings
a rock troll had left after squatting relief –
now crawling with tourists awing at its chance
moonscape, dark pools, inky lagoons,
anthropomorphic stones locked in craggy physiognomies –
one even scratched with King Oskar's signature –
and, lording over this vast labyrinth of stones,
stands Huss's statue, architect of blasted vision,
feet planted triumphant atop a lofty crag
perpetually surveying his breathtaking failure.

His spirit knows well a double-edged axiom:
some are born to failure, others have it blast upon them.

Driven in Sundsvall

...life is only comprehensible through a thousand... local gods.
... Worship... all you can see... and more will appear –
                                        Peter Shaffer, *Equus*

i.

Vast skies of Sundsvall sunder open,
sun shafts in, banishing shadows,
wrenching me from the comfortable dark
of thoughts' mushroom patch, cool introspection,
into sunburst of possibilities
petrified as the clutching trees,
the jagged stones, the terrible beauties,
the intensifying green in an unabashed sun,
that boundless sky, an atlas of sculptured cloud
depicting Nordic deities, storm-browed forebears,
billowing gods with sinewy limbs
in a tableau of grappled Giants,
mapped arbiters with epic brows,
translated mortals trumpeted
by raven-winged Valkyries.

ii.

And should I take that tumbling sky
and fold my arms around it
and scrunch the clouds into cotton balls
and stuff them in my sockets?

Should I, as a faint pain burrs inside
as if a poker skewers my brain,
throw out my arms and gather up
the tumbled sky, and start again?

Should I cauterise the beating sun
and pour its gold yolk down my throat?

iii.

Or maybe I should calm my mind
with thoughts on bed, its pillow-cold
cushioning solace, soft douse of fire
and fever searing through my boiled
metabolism like the over-heated
engine furring my hemmed-in feet
with burning vibes, a barely pent
polite insanity
fuelled on Englishness and tea –
what is this urge, this energy
vibrates through me but isn't in
my power to harness or determine?
Limp in the passenger seat, driven
by an unreasoning intensity
I have to create to alleviate.

iv.

On and on the storm-thoughts go.
We pass a turning to a town called Limbo.

v.

Your Scandinavian face aglow
in the gold sun of a sunlit churchyard;
a flash of the camera, a flash in me,
wanting to capture the moment for certain,
capture certainty, beat away
ambiguity; be lifted above
dead-ends, mazes and labyrinths leaning
in on themselves like beaten ambitions;
be freed from the sentence we all must bear;
drift into the light that is and isn't there.

vi.

In a second's camera flash you capture
panic in a snapshot, distracted
by your shining hair, blonde as a Bauer
angel, falling straw in the balm. I root
my thoughts once more in the ground, plant my
mind in the stony loam, lime-green, ragged.

vii.

I focus on the magic chapel
in a slate cap with a slatted steeple,
its rough-carved curvatures,
plain daubed white striated stem –
it's not been built but grown from the soil
like a toadstool, grown out of worship;
sprung up from nothing with the graves'
drunk tributes to planted spirits. Graves
they once called memory stones – I wish
my memories could be etched in stones
so I could put them down and walk away.

viii.

Nothing grows from nothing, yet it does.
No thought outlives itself, yet it tries.
A thought is an overgrown instinct, swollen
to poisonous ripeness like a ruby bane,
soon souring, overpowering its patch
till it has to be cut back.

              Calm again.
Mind drives away. Shadows and chapels
mushroom the pastures, patches of worship
spring all around on the rag-tag hills.

III

A Pageant of Abstracts

Where Banshees Brought Me

Gusts hurled blustery fists outside
　And threw, with sweeps, the rain
That lashed against the draughty glass
　Of the sunken window-pane;

I caught the squalling croon
　Of a thousand drowning choirs;
The bawling caterwauled across
　Plunging downs and dipping mires –

I heard them beckon me outside;
　Their morbid song, lifting in pitch,
Led me from a restive mood
　To the turbid depths of a ditch;

The wails turned to watery gasps –
　Into the ditch I tripped and fell;
The rain filled in the dug-up grave
　And there's little else to tell…

Except that here I drowned with ease –
　My thoughts: the bricks around this well.

The Shillelagh in the Corner's Eye

The shillelagh used to shout at me
from the corner of my perambulating eye,
from the cobwebbed corner of the cottage lounge,
crouched spider of spinning possibilities:
Come on, take my weight in your milksop hand…
Triggering threat in inanimate things
disturbing but benign, lodged like cudgels
in the mind besieged by flashes of acts
unconscionable – *I can be your liberation,*
limey – be your tool to smashing out the
smothering love in them! Shuddering sight:
the thought-out act seemed simple as spoon-
crushing the scalp of an egg-shell – but checked
emotions made it impossible: abhorrent.
Still the image cramped my head, crowded it out
with loved ones howling in their beds:
My God, what are you doing? You've gone mad!
Finally, finally, but only in my limbs'
interned twitches; phantoms of doubt;
no call for the Furies' haranguing this time,
I'm still in control – Gorgon-stoned by
proto-cognition – static as that
inanimate corner-dunce; that muttering shillelagh.

Adjusting the Heirloom

The static heaviness of home
like the thick, prickly atmosphere
before a thunderstorm.
Desperate strength to tug the mood
out of the tumbling dumps
minutely turns the weighty heirloom
an indiscernible inch
for the first time since time misremembers.
A lamp-lit glimpse
of new perspective faintly appears
in the half-moon of recusant dust
shadowing the base of the slightly shifted
object. Soon to be re-eclipsed
by love's scotched binds, memory prisms.
Trembling sentiment-malleable there,
thumping with ominous promise in
the mind's dorm like a rumbling migraine
on the brink of an all-out thunder.

A Chip in the Chippendale

No carpet on the floor.
No home comforts anymore.
Uncle's ormolu was sold
(Antique, so we were told).
A rusty heater fills the space
where it once took pride of place.
But it's still freezing here
so the sofa's huddled near.
Glad we've not yet passed the pale
to put the table up for sale:
my great grandfather's Chippendale.

Broke beside the heirloom
a door-knob wedged with a broom
battling with the fist
of a draught that will insist
as I sit here with wet hair
while the towel dries on the stair,
but it's just too damp to dry
though the heater is on high
and the light's about to fail
with one last sting in its tail:
we notice a chip in the Chippendale.

Charleston Pharaohs

Ours was an elastic home, it never broke – Quentin Bell

i. The Farmhouse Facade

A farmyard's straw and manure fades
as a painty fragrance wafts out through
the door to cool summoning glooms
of grey-faced Charleston's bracketed treasures,
glowing *Black Brook* shallows – warren
for a Singer Sargeant protégé
eloping with her brush and lover
to unfashionable chic *a la rustique*.

ii. The Tour

A whispery guide, reverential as if
curating relics of venerated Saints,
leads our trespass into the stilled head
of a dead Arts Hydra, up rackety stairs,
through corridors of paint-faded spoils left
by the Bloomsbury dynasty – Pharaonic
breed in turbans and flannel suits.
Their rooms, art deco tombs, assembled
by impulse, thrown like artists' parties;
colour-clashing slapdash affairs; rag-tag
gallimaufries – lamp-stands ad-libbed
from wastepaper bins in smoke-easy boudoirs
where writers, painters and flappers played.

Each crack, crease, crook, cross-stitch, mismatched
heirloom – Thackery's Dutch-walnut and
a marquetry table, damned to stilted smalltalk
like awkward party guests: a ramshackle
backlash at wallpaper pa's and gossamered
aunts. Duncan's strapping *au naturel* in oils
on an easel in *The Studio*, incarnadine
as the slapmark on 'good taste's' volte face.

iii. Part of the furniture

Maynard stayed so much a bedroom mushroomed
around him, where he moonbeamed on
macronomics on *the Morpheus' Bed*; and
in spite of mattress-spring ballerinas
(though he had Lopokova tucked up at home) –
the Bloomsbury bedroom farce – finished
The Economic Consequences Of The Peace.
A Delacroix pencil sketch, and a Cezanne
offloaded like luggage in a hedge at the end
of the lane – 'what a hoot' – equated to rent.

iv. Distinguished Guests

A laquered red cane decade clustered
round that dining table, a Camelot
of Bryllecreemed intellectuals rubbing
shoulders like the Staffordshire Figures
and gaudy Clarice Cliff pastiches
on the mantelshelf; sprays of caryatids
and stencilled chalk flowers on ash-black walls,
always alterable.   What arty tattle
they'd have ruminated through, freckled in
the rusticated light of an upturned strainer.

Taking cakes and ices in a glooming
garden room where saturnine Tom
first purred *April is the cruellest month…*
              Myopic Aldous tripping through
French windows of perception. The set's
sitting circle: Messrs Strachey and Saxon,
Miss Sitwell – lugubrious Virginia,
fidgetiest of sitters, captured
more lifelike in clay than in photograph:
a Gorgon bust *sans* snake-hair.
                        What paper
tales crackled in that rickety library
by the flickering *Cockerel and Dog*?

v. The Avant-Garden

Out in the avante-garden, chipped-nosed gods
cast marble stares from cobbled-flint walls
over statued lawns; a limpid pond
round as Omega dappled by lily pads
and dragonflies; a mossed ghost glowering up
from the rambling reeds at windows gulped
in shadows, walls scrawled with wisteria.

vi. Morpheus' Bed

The last-ditched front parlour, quieter than
its riotous cousins, where evenings grew.
A grubby Sickert miniature scowling on the wall
for a hint of urban grit. A pipe-and-slippered
abstract armchair against a pampering
of pastel lozenges along a makeshift mantle.
A book-cooled refuge of embrasured shade
from sunburned bohemian bonhomie...
Its reclusion shattered in a telegram:
the loss of one son besotted by poetry
and left-wing politics – dopes of the proles
and lower-middle-classes: taken out
in 'that blasted Spanish thing'; now, demobbed
and bootless upstairs on *the Morpheus' Bed*.

vii. After-facts

Heady days of painting, writing, thinking –
a rented farmhouse camouflage disguising
a singed paradise of otherworldly rooms,
now, wowing samplers for makeover vogue;
a museum of giving and letting go;
tombs to hoarded after-facts of empty-palmed Pharaohs
embalmed in objet d'art, sarcophagi of jumble,
absorbed back into the ebb and flow
of egoless objects: to be, but not to know.

Epigrams
for John Horder

Letting Go

Being: a long, surprise-filled haul
Of struggling, painful, slow –
Of coming to terms with coming to terms;
Of letting go of letting go.

The Marble Grave

He put a bit away for a rainy day,
His dictum, *it's always good to save* –
And when the rain came it pounded down
And marbled his marble grave.

Artist's Lot

The lot of the artist
Has always been rotten:
Be dead and remembered,
Or alive and forgotten.

Bronchial

If only I could cough up all my troubles
As easily as bile hits tissue –
But it's not the purging but the churning about
That is the real issue.

The End of the Metaphor

Should I, after tea and cakes and ices,
Have the strength to force the moment to its crisis?
                    T.S. Eliot, *The Love-Song of J. Alfred Prufrock*

The leaky pipe of the basement flat
boarded-up across the road
squeals and rustles like a tattle of rats.
I've stopped by the hand-spurned railings trailing
steps of brattling leaves to listen,
be convinced of no infestation.
An un-haunted mustard dark where ghost
recluses make their absence felt.

My nerves are elastic these rubbery days.
Scrap-paper trees stab antlers in the street
arcing the cat that talks by itself;
barbed shadows snag on the blistered beige
of terraces' burnt meringue.

Black tarmac glistens like a smoker's tongue
night-lit by lampposts that stub out the stars.
Where's that throaty singing tumbling from?
Something threading under the rain-pounded cars,
bobbing down the gutter like a buoy to the beat.
Ah! It's my head floating down the burst street.

O for thoughts to curl away
as coiled arabesques from a cigarette's stem.
Arbitrary light blasts the daily battlefield again.
Inner-enemies reassembling;
smoke-trolls amassing from ash hinterlands.
Thunder in the chest rumbles like an organ,
churns emphysema-hymns in the bronchia's
cathedral. In spite of distant artilleries
I roll and drill my rank-and-file
slim white infantries – then send
them one by one into the splutter of lungs.
There the metaphor must end.

Phantasms drag into partitioned day's
cramped flat: a gallery of damp and fags.
The goblin-green ghost of Harold Monro
hovers over my shoulder. I hope in time
ruminations' rioting patterns detach
from the thump of the mind, the spirit's split-
level; be separate as imprints, stripling
poems poured out in long bloomed youth.

Tonight I wrestle metaphors,
unlock inkhorns of Minotaurs.

The brain, a garbled labyrinth of honeycomb
abuzz with bee-thoughts stumbling by their stings
bumping off walls like balls of string.
As long as there are ropes, one copes. Dreams bland
unbearable day. The sinking pillow
whispers escape but morning gropes
soon one un-puffs its battered cloud.
One vague future day all there'll be is the bed
sighing your imprint: a urine shroud.

Since a child I've plunged in imponderables,
dabbled in abstractions the brain can't contain:
eternal light, blindness, oblivion. Nerves'
swell peddles pump purple dread at unending
dark, the sealed lid. — But I begrudge
the blind man's cloak of peacock tones; his wombed
solipsism. The heart's fleshy clock beats time;
each tock-thought, a sweaty-palmed haul up the bend
in slippery banisters, a hesitation
on the stairs. There the metaphor must end.

Vintage

Nose-bleed spoor of an awful wine,
uncultivated, vindictive, cheap,
with a hint of the plummy unmentionable
puddles my lamp-punished desk,
moats the plinth of an ashtray charred
by black thumb-prints – this vicious wine:
perfect complement to blue
cheese, red meat, fluoxetine.

My parched throat's tickled by nicotine,
voice rasping; ash-blasted tongue
brackish with tar. Corked thoughts clogged
with bottlestops of doubt. Sour tang
of phlegm emerges cramping breaths
while lungs like flapping mackerels
gasp to understated deaths.

Posterity's bottle may mature to adage;
and a dusty vintage.

Suddenly Thunder
for LMB

Suddenly, it ended like a heatwave:
a sky's impermeable blue bruised by
one thunderburst ousting the heaviness
so long stored – struck in a flash to muggy
concussion. A narrative built up to
patter out to limp impasse on the page.
    Now I wake to a sun's cloudy yolk
casting faint albumen on light-bulb days;
draw the curtains until night shrinks in.
Oh, I go out – but only to trace back. I'll
turn the corner, or think I have, gaze
up at a gap-light in the drapes of the flat,
half-expecting to find you curled upstairs
in the couch, *mi gata*, like a cat.
    I haunt the faded afternoons
of traceless past, once tangible
as these vague laughterless rooms
I grope in through gradual marbling pain,
clouding to dull rumble, purring to dark.
    Absently, I replace your traces
with ill-matched miniatures, bric-a-brac
to stamp a heart's dismantling; things
only *my* sentiments have invested in.
    Nights scratch nests from under-cliffs
of pillows, for the thousandth forgetting
before plunging to sleep. You'll appear
in dreams imparting small details of your
new life; we'll reflect, merge tones once more
like colour-echoes in a daubed Cezanne;
your tapering hands will brush mine for last
as a shadowy warmth waves us apart.
    Feels like only yesterday, last week:
you reaching the end of a novel in bed –
buenos noches y dulces suños said
as I kissed your quail-egg cheek –
you turning the pages in your head,
whispering, *how suddenly it ended*.

Tomorrow Will Be Another Day
For LMB

I'm haunted by what you used to say,
How harmless but sad it used to sound:
Tomorrow will be another day.

You took a half of me away
And left your ghost to keep me bound.
I'm haunted by what you used to say.

At some point we both lost our way;
A cloud shadowed our common ground.
Tomorrow will be another day.

I couldn't keep the stars at bay;
You couldn't hide your hopes were downed.
I'm haunted by what you used to say.

I fill the space where you once lay
With warming emptiness unbound.
Tomorrow will be another day.

It seems like only yesterday
New love was lost, old doubts were found.
I'm haunted by what you used to say.
Tomorrow will be another day.

Last Laughter

After Laughter

I remember when I first knew her
            – and after:
God, the voice of an angel –
            that laughter…

Dark Laughter

Funny how laughter
when it turns hysterical
resembles crying.

Laughter in the Bathroom

I catch your laughter in the mirror's shatter,
your ghost reflection in the splintered glass –
snatch after-trace of your barefoot patter,
miss the hiss of days wash in and pass.

Echoes from the bathroom, a thrashing tail
of laughter caught in water, splashing louder –
then silent. A damp towel dashed on the rail.
A second pair of footprints in the talcum powder.

Oxide Yellow Minor

...it is one of the chief purposes of decoration... that it has
to sharpen our dulled senses: for this end are those wonders
of intricate patterns interwoven, those strange forms invented –
                    William Morris, *The Decorative Arts*, 1877

Behind closed lids deep indigo night
(Reflections from veins in the retina?)
I see William's crawling wallpaper,
Unfathomable foliage, cerebrum-white:

Tortuous intricacies; inner-sight
Inverted: blue-touch tendrils taper,
Lobed leaves sprout like the brain's cauliflower–
Optics lost to Catherine-wheels of light:

Acanthus, raging Marigold, sharp bite
Of Apple, fiery Honeysuckle, Larkspur,
(Ripostes to Brinton's rioting of Kiddiminster)
Tangible slide effects from the bakelite

Sanity of Lustral, its coursing sertraline –
Vegetable palate of the dye-refiner:
Weld yellow, red madder, indigo carmine,

Iron oxide black – produces a shiner
For bruising senses: the brilliantine
Curlicues of Oxide Yellow Minor.

[Note: Brinton of Kiddiminster was a contemporary designer of Morris's, whom the latter considered the producer of tasteless patterns].

Gulliver Head

for Sally Richards

When I broke out from Lilliput
Escaped my giant thrall
And found my way back to five foot seven small
I found that oddly my mighty thoughts
Had remained the same size as in Lilliput
Where an accident of scale by chance
Had aggrandized my stride in all things
Having to be careful not to tramp cities
And people on my wanderings –
As, when a baby, I'd crawled across my
Brother's cardboard castle, crushing its turrets;
My thoughts had outgrown vicinities
I once fitted into, and were growing still –
Things would never be the same size again;
Looking at everything around me
Through the wrong-end of the lens
As when an adult you drift to revisit
Those vast haunts of childhood's stomping grounds
Now suddenly seeing how small and cramped
And easily trampled they really are.

Knights in Taut Castles

[adj. obsessed from the Latin *obsessus*: besieged]

Thoughts cram the taut castle.
Over-sized Knights and Knaves jostle
cluttering tiny turrets,
cramping miniature battlements…
towers, so out of proportion.

Claustrophobic chivalry.

Sword and shield pyramid
in slopes to absolutes –
scrunched by tempests to crumpled tents
but still incarcerating sense.

The enemy gathers invisibly.
The oil boils over the battlements
relentlessly under siege…

Obsessing Room Only, my liege.

Kink Knut

Rootless, since memory imprisoned me:
at ten loosed from ties into superstitious
Cornish backwaters. Ten month's off school
for intrusive thoughts, driven reclusive.
Innocent to the stamp of stagnation
gathering to darker fantasias:
picturing posthumous futures, absent
but aware, a ghost among my mourners.

The waters lash in and I lash back.

Melding identity with lumpen parents,
aping a father's Somerset past
as a boy at Rock; cramming my room
with peeling barks of crinkled spines
crookbacked on the speckled shelf;
paper knights galloping allegro;
Holst's striding *Jupiter* thumping in
the stirrup-spiriting afternoon.

I lash at the waters and they lash back.

Deep-slipping, absenting bliss;
tadpole circling out of pond-context,
brined in frogspawn of pause; aspic
of limbo. Buried in undefined
countryside's timeless rolling rills.
Blurring boundaries: day, night, youth, age –
tumbling into one on the page.

The waters lash in and I lash back.

Happy in absolutes, absently bartering:
'If I sacrifice this, I can have that…'
balancing scales, tilting at tipping
into soul-floored slump. Haunting the day,
a contented shadow in intrepid strides

of an older sibling. Solo, unschooled
but for thumbprints on sprays of uniforms
or ghostly plates' static chivalries.

I lash at the waters and they lash back.

An Anti-Knut: a kink in my thinking,
hand raised to halt mutating waters,
stall time's tide wrapping round the legs
of my capsizing chair, convinced
I'm still King of my thinking, Prince
of scraping precocities, while my
courtiers see me knotting, sinking…

My mind pulled under, I grope through leather
sargasso for sturdier ties to take root –
new title to tilt with: Kink Knut.

IV

Tracing the Pattern

Bosham Tides

Rebounded, in mumbling summer
to Bosham, your favourite bygone haunt,
that last stop on our move to Cornwall's
dark, back in Nineteen Eighty-Five...
Today, a nostalgia trip, sipping tea
in that same 'oldie-worldie' café
with pillars crimped like pasty crusts
and walls patterned like marble cake –
a gallimaufry of mistake.

In the cool of the sand-coloured Saxon church
we perch on pews. You almost comment
'It's nice here', or something similar –
it doesn't really matter what you said,
just that you tried to say it.

We stay staring at the vacant altar
instead of scraping down to the crypt.

Out in the shrinking light, we watch
the cloudy shallows lap the walkway –
the boundary between land and sea
bruising more with each tidal mark –
I picture Canute with warding hand
failing to halt the crawling waters
as your coursing thoughts wash in and out
fizzling off on a sandy vagueness.

Canute wasn't here in historical fact,
and you come and go with the tides.

Mermaids' End

In the pea-green nursing home
a future shadowed the wall:
all leads to this dead-end –
life, then death, that's all;
nothing to come afterwards,
no haloed reward, no welcoming
from a dumb other side – only this:

thrown into an unfamiliar armchair
scented with other people,
fragrances of impersonal sprays
characterless as the dead –
the kitsch serge of seats without souls
bleached and sanitised parade
stuffing-knocked ragged dolls.

She's having one of her bad days
understates the cloth-faced nurse
her tone in-tune with gaudy décor,
mannerly flowers on drab wallpaper.

Dead verbs drop like watered-down
doses of medicine falling useless
in brine-dark tonic ebbing from
the coiled old lady's tearless eyes
shielded by tissue-crumpled hand
craned against her egg-shell brow;
knotted in a chair, varicose shins
ending in green slippers beached like a clump
of seaweed on the sandy carpet,
splayed as a mermaid's tail.

So it is: the upholstered dead-end,
final insult to the spirit's immortal
fancies, tall-tail stories that talked us
into staying, only to take
away hereafters after waiting's pain.

It all ends here with washed-up laughter,
tears, desires, ambitions, dreams,
loves, hates, album-memories –
into the cul-de-sac of wrinkled scales,
sagging fins and tightening gills.

The insipid painting of boiled green seas
against an impossible cornflower sky
salvaged on the hallway wall –
nothing like the choppy grey that beats nearby.

Saint Vitus's Dance

Once she was able to say Yes –
could mouth life's affirmation without
a quiver of doubt –
now she spills just *Yawf, yawf, yawf* –
pale spell to reassure,
mantra for thought-cushioning –
to ward off thorny worrying;
sped up, Professor Yaffle's patter:
Yaff, yaff, yaff – but in sticking time's
stylus-scratch, trips out as… *Yawf*…

Sometimes this stifled Yes is paired
with *Yawfit, yawbit, bawfit, boffit* –
Tolkien-fangled tongue, to say
Stop it – That's it – Hoppit – Hobbit…
Half-swallowed vowels go down the wrong way,
gristly verbiage sticks in her throat; face
crowds out with twitches, empties with clenches:
jaw clamped in bruxism's vise.

My mind flashes to cold photos of cavities
unambiguously black, vital grey membranes
eaten away, the irreplaceable grapes
of the basal ganglia going slowly sour;
brain ravaged to rotten cauliflower.

Teeth and tongue trip elocution
that schooled her Eliza Doolittle
groomed from Manor House council stables
to treading the boards, a yawning age ago.
Now she's tutored in smudged speech seeded
in dud genes' dominos; a slur
of lines, rehearsed parlance for clunking
curtain call, retched theatrical;
her gait, no more days' gone adagio,
now locked in Saint Vitus's jolting dance.

[*bruxism*: clenching and grinding of teeth].

Wax like Fragile Daylight

Sunlight was discouraged: it fades the draperies.
                    Bill Turner, 'Homely Accommodation, Suit Gent'

i.

To always want to be somewhere else,
anywhere but wherever here is –
eyes' each yolky albumen
developing a special lens
grasping in transparency
of grainy unreality
displaced as moments' crockery
shaking in the tap-dripped sink.

Lights make movements, shadows morph
to people, shadow people who
morph back to shadows, theatrical
tricks of chilling chiaroscuro…

How to know day from night,
light from dark, when never quite
asleep or awake? Always trapped
in a drowsy dream-belt…

Is someone outside in the broken eggshell light
of the net-curtains' fracturing?
Is that one of your shadow sons visiting? Leaving?
(Are people simply memories
Frankensteined in time's stitching?).

See Time for the trickster It is:
tack and inanimate
faking painted happiness –
things are laughing at us.

ii.

You suspect we're ghosts orbiting
your only mind, unsettling
solipsism sinks in the missing settee…
only you are left behind
haunted by paper-traced impostors –
you see through us all; at times, even doubt
your own foggy contours.

Wrung from mourning others –
a cat, two dogs, your cancer-faced friend –
scraps left to anticipate something
future past, safer pre-bereaved.
Funerary years haven't been kind,
threaten to trip again any moment;
lampshade Harpies grabbing at
gradually granulating darlings.

Better interpret all as already
absent, so no more loss to fear.
The toll of the phone might as well be a sign
from the other side as the end of a line.

Harold of the chorea – feather in trilby –
chair-bound Beryl, Aunties Doff
and Olive, Uncles Sid and Ernie,
all late, sat in this lounge with leaden
stares; shades from your pencilled-in mind
easily smudged, rubbed out.

iii.

When Dad's out you miss his duck-egg grey
freckled haunting, fear even his ghost
may fade, wax like fragile daylight
then wane to pale assurances –
a chip-toothed Cheshire Cat leaving
the trace of a crumbling smile.

Brief relief to the hum of his car
hovering into the drive. For seconds,
spared from yourself. A wax hand peels
the curtain, then sinks feather-light
back to its time-warped perch:
shiver of lace on a faded chair-arm.

The Moth and the Song Thrush

When mother shot into my bedroom
In the inky early hours, night-blind,
Confused as to where she was, as I,
It reminded me of that cottage morning
I'd woken in rickety summer to spy
A huge shape flapping across my room
And out onto the landing – a moth,
I'd thought, of abnormal scale, as I
Slammed my bedroom door shut till
It settled leaf-like to shiver on a wall…
But it turned out to be a song thrush morphed
Through the bars of my sleep-blurred eyes.
Natural things can, when trapped in a room,
Seem an unnatural size.

The Sunsetters

Remarking a translucent peach sky ahead,
a Turner-scape traced by the hesitating sun,
we reflected on mum's receptiveness that visit.

At one amber moment, my eyes caught hers
glowing with nostalgic vigour, a glint
goldening her brown pupil, so long fogged

by mood-clouding pills; now, for one moment
she shone through the dark, warmly smiling.
Then the glint dimmed back to chalky vague.

Gone, that moment, that one sunny break
in a cloud of blunted brow. Back to
the blank mask pattered invisibly

by anxiety's muffled batteries;
wheezes like Heaven's artilleries.
No traceable signs. Nerves shattered by

a silencer. Shapeless shrapnel lodged
like lead in the eyes. But, sure enough,
vestiges of her abeyant fire

flared back at Graylingwell – the daily
last stand of her feistier-self;
a sign, we clutched, she might re-emerge…

I built up my hopes as we, the sunsetters,
rode back admiring dusk's deepening peach;
blushes of rouge behind clawing trees.

Yes, it's beautiful but not a good sign
sighed dad at the wheel, a thrum of thunder
catching in his throat. Beyond the orange glow
grey was bruising in. *Bodes storms tomorrow.*

Now Barabbas…

What did you have for lunch today?

– *I don't know*

You had roast chicken, didn't you?
And treacle pudding and custard.
What's the day today?

– *I don't know*

It's the same as any other day.
What did you do yesterday?

– *I… saw my sons*

No, that was the day before, wasn't it?
What did you eat yesterday?

– *I don't know*

We had salad.
Who was Jesus crucified in place of?

– *Barabbas…*

Tracing the Pattern

...when you follow the lame uncertain curves for a little distance they suddenly commit suicide -- plunge off at outrageous angles, destroy themselves in unheard of contradictions   – Charlotte Perkins Gilman, *The Yellow Wallpaper* (1899)

1.

She inhabits a dark night of the sole
in fuggy corridors of Graylingwell
carpeted to soften thought –
tripping in dull-thudding dark
absented in haze, past, present glazed,
haunted by nun-habits, convent school shades.
Should she resign from the nursing home
         she left strung years ago?
Still haunted by lifting and handling,
stoning chores that frayed her flint
in auxiliary past, blunting it.
It's too uncanny – this clotted detour.
And isn't Richmond the Avenue
they ambulanced from to treat her here?
It must have been.

2.

This time: the patient, shuttered in
with slipper-wearing wraiths
for cross-symptoms of Huntington's:
no fitting limbo to billet this
         memory evacuee,
so improvise through postcode bingo;
         label lottery.
She goes outside, but supervised.
Her skipping feet know off by heart
each dip and rise of their daybeat.

Only the fag-yellowed Miss Havisham
cobwebbed in smoke and dandelion-clocks
– who squawks like a parakeet – is forgotten
among the lilies and forget-me-nots.

3.

Twig-fragile on the crackling phone
Trappist-silent ruminations
tap spine-chills. Spectral breath
prickles the nape of my neck:
telepathic cross-correspondence,
plunge of the gut, tug of the soul
to the breathily whispered dread –
made real if spoken, like a spell;
empathy trembles in postponed
       thanatophobia…
They're dead. They're really ghosts. I think
I've already died. No point in visiting.
I'll have to resign…

4.

I grasp her sharper past mind-tight
but the grains spill into misted vague
       snapshots of personality
now wallpapered up, trapped in tapering
sulphur-yellow patterns, shapes,
       curlicue suicides,
tasteless arabesques turning the stomach,
scraping the fabric of sanity…

5.

If only we'd read the signs: Swandean
            sapping her appetite,
difficulties swallowing for apple-core thoughts
lodging in her swan-down throat;
phobias slippery as tallow soap;
sponge-nerves, insights in disguise
too mighty to be extinguished by talk.

6.

Easy to trace the pattern once formed –
            then no unravelling.
Hindsight's a burdensome thing:
late knowledge of Huntington's
honeycombing her brain –
            the bee's tail-sting.
Time waits for her thoughts to bed down.
Too late for stripping the wallpaper,
            its pattern's long set in.
Her grasp of the real now shaved paper-thin.
But then in time they'll try untangling
the coiled springs of her thinking.

7.

At least she's in the safest place
to look for herself again.

The photographed doctor in clouds and khakis
stares out on his wards beatifically.

In   Carnations

I walked with her,   talked with her
without being there   just one of my
faint incarnations'   soothing words
echoing her head   round ghostly grounds
of crematorium-quiet   Graylingwell

on half-suggested paths   by emptying meadows
pastel-brick labyrinths   boarded-up stucco
Georgian wards   white-gravel drives
dream-scattered annexes   Austenite pilasters
thought-pausing porticos   waiting, waiting

for ghosts to come haunt   with old pillow hopes
thought long ago gone   but all this time hidden
just round the bend   by sand lawns, hydrangeas,
carnations, paused plants slipper-parted grasses

from Richmond Avenue   to Richmond Ward…
Has it all been a dream…? *Has it…in the end?*
Peace stilled in absence   of needling questions
no weeding need   for stitching answers
softly detouring   calm, in carnations.

V

A Tapestry of Absent Sitters

Raging Grains
for Simon Jenner

Dust-deep, lime-curtained, labyrinthed in
blanched prints and sun-published spines,
Hobbit of the cubby-holes and foxed metaphors
inspecting your perfect-bound regiments drilled
in dark kitchen cupboards glued to attention
for tunic inspection. You introduced me
to future-thumbed numbers of posthumous lodged
in your stucco pad's book-wombed spare room.

Got to know broke John, whose thirty bob a week
barely kept him dapper in his dog-eared flaps,
just scraping by to share a shilling's worth
of rhotic ectoplasm trailing like lime-scale
in the kettle crusted with greening litotes.
Shook hands with Harold, a dour sottish cove,
whose none-too-silent pool of only observations
peeved us high on dipsomania; choked
crimson with glottal hiccoughing for
his bottlestopped catamite tendencies.

You corked a rosé, poured three glasses when
Bernard, Muse-commuter, missed his train.
Thought we'd make a night of it therefore
and toasted his de-railed posterity.
Apparently they found him stretched on the rails
in Vienna – a faulty carriage door?
PINSTRIPED MYSTERY... And tumbled Alun,
heaped by his pluming revolver in Burma.

Shame I missed short-notice Clifford drop by –
he was gone at the first flash of day – but I
picked through the scraps he left, straight or curly.
Struck lucky that time khaki Keith unpacked
his kit-bag of sand grains and aphorisms
still yet to be simplified, now he was dead.
All this time Sidney K jangled keys on the stairs.

Can't repay you for these chance introductions
to such sub-tenanting literati
immaculately jacketed in time-scale rinse.
Spiders sent crawling across the page
ink-scratch incantations in their names;
nib-tributes to faded cream-papered Fabers'
saddle-stitched staple. Onion-skinned shades
indelibly Brailled on raging grains.

[Key to poets: 'broke John', John Davidson; 'Harold' Monro; 'Bernard' Spencer; 'Tumbled Alun' Lewis; 'short-notice Clifford' Dyment; 'Sidney K' (Keyes); 'khaki Keith' Douglas].

Mister Aspidistra
i.m. Harold Monro (1879-1932)

Hobo of broadsides, goblin contradiction
Among sunning Georgians. Absence-in-
Residence: poet and shopkeeper. An
Obiter dictum in the blasting storm; gloom-
Lyrics aslant the lightning rain. Foxed and
Dog-eared, my copy of his orange volume.

Moon-eyed, mustachioed, souped in lapels; an
Oaky vintage with hint of manila and
Nicotine on his tongue's bitter sanctuary.
Reclusive chaperone of shop-curtains, smiling
Out with stiff soldierly bows, a slight wave.

The Vulnerable Stag
i.m. John Davidson (1857-1909)

Jago poet, twitching pen-hand on the pulse
Of poverty; scribbled nerve unswerving,
Hacking out a coughing crust. *Mal de moderne,*
Neurasthenia, his rummiest Testament.

Dragger of dromedaries, trappings of family,
Asthmatic stag caparisoned with lions.
Vulnerable to rubs; prickly to critics;
Irascible antlers snagged by every barb.
Drubbed balladeer in a hump. Rag wage
Snatched by lightning rent for rooms like travel trunks.
O for the fire of Blake to raze these grubby slums.
No cure for hypochondria, cancer or Penzance.

[*rummiest*: of or like rum; some phrases in this poem allude to Davidson's
famous ballad, 'Thirty Bob A Week']

Hay Bails and Short Straws

i.m. Thomas Hardy (1840 – 1928)

Time's amanuensis, savant of the Fates,
Hay-bailed to Nature's Tantalus ways;
Oracular badger brindled by bait's
Moon-beamed betrayal in the henge's rigged rays;
Architect of rustic myth, arbitrary traits
Scattered like dandelion-clocks on rocked days.

Hubris-blunter for hutched pariahs
Aspirant in class-traps; scribe of short straws
Ravelling Shalt Knots round Christminster spires;
Digger of tragedies. Heart nabbed by paws –
Yolked to frumenty in a cat's snatching jaws.

[*frumenty*: a dish of hulled wheat boiled in milk and seasoned with sugar, cinnamon, and raisins. Michael Henchard in Hardy's *The Mayor of Casterbridge* laced his frumenty with alcohol, with tragic results].

Trampler in the Patchwork
i.m. Gerrard Winstanley (1609-76)

Grown from the common soil, crop-haired, green
Egalitarian, made of clod and light,
Rainbow-sown. A trampler in the patchwork:
Raking the scrublands only God the One True
Absentee Landlord could snatch from our hearts.
Recalcitrant in tracts, your flat-crowned, felt-shaded
Diggers set to work to till the natural law.

Withstanding the dirt of labour's nagged brow,
Impeachments of coin-palmed Parliaments,
Nettling barbs of vigilantes' abuse – your
Spade-handed disciples disbanded,
Threw down their shovels on a chapter versed
Against the grain of transplanted times:
New tyrannies travelled on trade winds. True
Leveller, tripping your ungrounded age,
Elevated above the hedges, those berries
You reached for are ripening on the page.

[*Rainbow* is also an allusion to radical Thomas Rainborow, or Rainsborough, whose name varied in spelling.]

Jack of the Bean-Straw

i.m. John 'Free Born' Lilburne (1615-1657)

Jack-in-the-Pulpit of political cloth, pumped
Out Puritan agitprop – lashed at a cart-tail:
He'd know the allegations in his mother tongue,
No trumpery in pope-speak for Free Born John.

Labelled agitator by parliaments of owls;
Inflammatory tracts and pamphlets, pettifogged.
Levellers, so-called, petitioned in his name;
Bonny Besses in sea-green dresses slinging hail-shot
Under Roundheads' squibs. Root and branch ripped out.
Radicals dispatched at churchyards. Ribbons banned.
Nothing for it but a trade, burn of kelp and bean-straw:
England's Birthright scrubbed by a soap-boiler's hands.

[*pettifogged*: an old word for quibbling or chicanery. Note: last line alludes
to Lilburne turning to the trade of soap-boiling (making soap), though he
later resumed his radical pamphleteering, ending his days in and out of
prison].

Asgill Translated

to my translated ancestor, John Asgill (1659–1738)

Tell me, maverick ancestor, were you snatched in
Rapture at the end? Did you finally translate
According to the Covenant you cited in your
Notorious tract, burnt by the hangman? Just the
Salient points of your impeached pamphlet that
Led arraigning Parliaments to expel you: an
Argument divine fusion happens in a flash, a
Translation to the immortal world 'without the
Experience of death' once one thinks like the in-
Dwelling spirit of God. We can depart before death.

Alas, this vague descendant's inherited a less
Scholastic take on death, more a morbid itch to
Grasp at any scraps that might bar it. So *if* there
Is an escape clause from the mortal cul-de-sac,
Like a cloud with a porter to transport him, do
Let him know the protocol as soon as you can.

[Note: the subject of this poem and some lines herein are drawn from
John 'Translated' Asgill's 1770 pamphlet: *Argument proving that, according
to the Covenant of Eternal Life revealed in the Scripture, Man may be translated
from hence into that Eternal Life without passing through Death* – for which he
was expelled from both the English and Irish Parliaments].

Light Shining in Lanarkshire

i.m. Keir Hardie (1856–1915)

Knock, knock! The baker's boy, sharp as clocks back,
Ear to the pithead's cogs – upturned prams spun
In puddles. By ten, melts in with clogging ranks:
Resurfacing day-shadows scrubbing home to tubs.

His pit-lamp halos pin-scratched Pitman in lit
Anticlines. Cage-clattered up strata on a carbon
Ribbon to paper and Party. — In the after-
Damp of Parliament's scalds, he signs off under
Inked portcullis; packs up his kit, books and cough;
Ebbs back to shadow. But his shadow casts a light.

[Mining terminology: *anticlines* arches or folds in layers of rock shaped like crests of waves; *cage* conveyance used to transport men and equipment in a shaft; *afterdamp* a toxic mixture of gasses left in a mine following an explosion].

Ragged Rob
i.m. Robert (Noonan) Tressell (1870–1911)
author of *The Ragged Trousered Philanthropists* (1914)

Robert who? Croker? Noonan? Tressell? Alter-ego
Owen? Journeyman between midstairs and downstairs.
Blacklisted decorator of camouflaged class. Self-
Evicted from kin-in-kind to a landlord's absent shadow.
Rough tobacco and adulterated tea: his tub-thumped
Turps-tin epithets.   — O for a *Sholes & Gidden*:

Tortuous long-hand manuscripts rejected, unread.
Ragged trails of scribbled drafts trousering his bed to
Edited ends. Mugsborough mug, tached and trilby'd in
Sixpence ha'penny suit, bannered on tubercular red.
Shabby genteel, rung-skidder anti-Kipps-wise, but
Earned a dying: signwriter turned writer of the times.
Labour's landslide, '45: owed to his bold novel?
Laid to rest, not the less, with twelve tramps, in Liverpool.

[Note: Tressell lived for a time in South Africa, where he had a manservant of whom he was very fond, whom he called 'Sixpence'. *Turps*: abbreviation for turpentine. *Sholes & Gidden* was an early make of typewriter.]

Ravelling Williams
i.m. Ralph Vaughan Williams (1872–1958)

Rapt in his green-sleeved valleys, cascading
Arcadias of choral walls – *O Clap Your Hands!* –
Largos, galloping folk songs, fantasias,
Pastorals khaki – *Bonny Boy* Albion regained:
His vistas of gavotting verdant strides.

Variations on a theme of blasted times
Amplified in brasses, peace's soft-pedalled
Uncertainties – swagger cane bartered for baton
Grasped to gather quivered wheat of flailing song
Harvested with barleycorn; steep falling away
And rising like waving dales. Shelled ruins in
No-man's-land: his coral landscape flared at dusk.

Wader in the green demi-paradise old Gaunt
Idealised; Hardy patch-worked with the Fates.
Light and leaden eyes of pale pencilled grey
Like our plunging skies, rough blustery seas
Incarnated in symphonies travelling from
Abroad: Ravel's vantage carved an island voice.
Magical, his craggy gryphon face vast-scaled as
Sweeping spells conducted by his ravelling wand.

The Lion of Pontrhydyfen
i.m. Richard Burton (1925–1984)

...to obviate the idea of the richness and extraordinary beauty of the world,
I thought it was best to leave it...   – Richard Burton, 1974

Roman bust on barrow shoulders,
marble-sculpted mouth and brow,
leonine; stabbing blue-fire stare –
two Satanic labradorites.

Trajan's face reincarnate
as a pitted Co-Op pulpit boy
into a flinty mining village
choked in pits and damp-steamed hills.

Voice awash of ash and granite
splashing anger, rasping rage –
now vanquished angel's caterwaul –
now hounded scowling howl –
now stone-intoning chapel roll
grafted on the thumping page.

Flame blazed out like *Zanzibar*...
Cormorant... on his scorched tongue
singed by tar and brackishness;
a barstool bard of verbalese
in drink's slow, slurring suicide
to obviate the richness...

Visage, vodka-ravaged to
cratered moonscape, wasted cast
quarried out of rakish fame's
encrusted spine, harsh fags;
roar tamed to a smoky growl...
pockmarked god with white-licked sides;
a lion snarling its last gasped drags.

Hare

Spring-limbed sprinter of Lepus
be born fur-coated, lozenges open –
saccadic ebons trapped
in stark-staring ambers;
hind legs bucked, sprung catapults.
Sharp-listening twitcher in the thickets,
taciturn watcher in prating nature
– shy as the skies, un-graspable in grass,
skimming the swaying vision-field.
Be fast as racing waters, fast
as definition's flicking lash –
ready to rear up for sporting box
mitts fisted in March fracas, balm-raving,
braced for opportunity's knocks:
razor-whiskered competition,
nose-knitting, teeth-smiting, staring-out games.
No shelter from nature's laissez faire;
no safety in numbers, only in pairs,
or opt-out solitaire;
no place to rest save an ill-hid nest
or shallow hollow. Skimp, scrape, scamp,
moonlight or borrow, scarper your share;
never late, always sharp, daylight may wait;
never still; no time to pay, save, hate;
only the flitting shimmer of sun
chases your sprint, harassed Hare;
darting all your days till time-light
whitens your buff-brown coat,
nibbles down your tall dapper ears
to split-end sheaves, twine-bandaged as
Tenniel's caricature.   Then, brittle-
limbed, bow out brave quarreller with Time,
lay down your wicker-light skull
bound liberated into the unthreading
of those stitched-on amber eyes.

[Note: John Tenniel (1820 – 1914): illustrator of Lewis Carroll's *Alice* stories]

Acquired Tastes

Being: a temperamental, appley wine.
Its effect, not instant, takes bearding time
To filter through. First nausea sets in.
But the more one sips, a seeping-in
Of warmth, hope, berried resignation.
Then acquire its taste, peregrination
Of sapping buds – leads to a wander
Round rich fruits; pained asunder
Of flesh. The business of existence based,
Not on instinct, beliefs, desires – but taste.
That bittersweet tang came from an apple –
Or grape? All fruits windfall in chapel.
Some sip the wine, keep sipping still.
Some, after one, know they've had their fill.

At Ambleside

Hartley Coleridge to Branwell Brontë

Dear *Branwell*

That day at Ambleside my friend
where we both laid our failures,
unassailable ambitions,
like feathers onto water
to drift invisibly forever,
was as well for me a small warm summer
in the Titan stride of winter –
we have shared, I feel, an interlude
of kindred respite, a meeting and
intermingling of minds,
a mirroring of moments,
a marriage of reflections.
Know thyself, the philosophers say,
and by knowing you for only hours
I find for the first time I am nearer
to knowing that life-shy inner-me
that least of all I ever see –
as for my aspect, I suspect
that was, in all its curiousness
(I mean my prematurely white
old man's mane, autumnal gait
and jittery disposition), some-
thing of a disappointing sight.
It's also one that contradicts,
as if by inverse caricature,
my juvenile green heart:
yes you may laugh at this, but I
still believe I cannot die –
an infantile immortal sense
I know the want of pains your soul
for what choice have you but to know
your time is limited, shall stop,
with graves crowding your window?
But I can tell you life is more

unbearable without an end
in sight; it's like an endless day
un-punctuated by the dark
that multiplies abundantly.
And so that's why my hair grows white
while I'm still fairly young:
because it's not had any nights,
nor has been spared of sun.
Well, my fellow Halfling friend,
my red-maned kin-diminutive,
it seems we both are as thin-skinned
as crinkled apples felled by wind –
I'll ask for last that you forgive
the letter I will never send.

Hartley

p.s. – your 'marbled skies',
I truly loved your 'marbled skies'.

The Ghosts of Haworth

'Let's see if one tree won't grow as crooked as another, with the same wind to twist it'. – Heathcliff in Wuthering Heights *by Emily Brontë*

i.

Storming thoughts
no stones unturned
mice-feet pace
the ringing table
tossing minute-
scripted stories
to Lilliputians
in the country of Wainscot –
rustle of hems
shingle of hemp
hissing the parsonage floor –
Banshees of Haworth
casting small shadows
green to pen spells
dashing a quarry
in sheets' sweat and writhing.

ii.

Anne: We once had a brother called Branwell, I'm sure.
Emily: Our variable brother Branwell.
Charlotte: Variable even down to his hands,
          each gifted its own prehensile will:
Anne: …to draw with the right, and write with the left
Emily: …the scratch of the pencil, the crack of the quill
Charlotte: …our ambidextrous brother…
Emily: …a double-tasking marmoset…
Anne: …a triple-headed prodigy…
Charlotte: In his place now seethes a ramshackle ghost
          trapped between limbo and this cold shattered place.
Anne: We warned him not to fall between four stalls.
Emily: But he showed not the same fleet-feet as when
          he'd scamp over the gravestones.

Charlotte: His sweat's all a-chill beading the rims
        of his wire eyes
Anne: – Hush! He might catch our whispers upstairs
        and think them Banshees' wassailing hushaby's…
Charlotte: He doesn't know whether he haunts
Emily: …or is haunted…
Anne: …as the wind knows not whether
Emily: …it blows or is blown.
Charlotte: The word *infernal* is branded on his brow,
        its letters patterned from the pox.
Anne: He who is no longer who he was born.
Emily: Thrown back to thunder from where he was torn.
Anne: Poor, poor Branwell.
All: Infernal… Eternal…
Anne: …tangled in bracken like a stag snagged by darkness
Emily: …on the winnowing moor…
        [*Nine 'o' clock rap on the door:*]
Patrick: Good night my children – don't stay up too late…

iii.

Taciturn Patrick
paternal jackdaw
breaks the silence of his beak
with habitual caw
muffled behind his neckerchief,
its inching swaddling of his chin
the tidal mark his miniature daughters
use to tell the shored-up years
moaning through the dolls' house rafters…

Haloed in candle-glow
up the wooden hill
the myopic Parson follows the shadow
of a giant crow.

The ragged stairs creak,
the banisters groan –
boughs of a dark wood.

Don't stay up too late –
incantation to grate
at the insatiable chirruping
of paper creations.

iv.

Too late for the family's Chatterton
cliffed upstairs, impatient for
failure – the artist's thrall;
banished, obscured, knowing his shadow
will cast no further than the lamp-dabbed wall
(where 'the abdabs'' little people crawl),
no trace of his gifts to out-trace him;
paints himself out from among his kin;
a ghost in the cracks on the canvas.

Charlotte: Trampled by scattering talent
Emily: …too wilful, too fiery, too green
Anne: …nerves too rickety, under-ripe,
            to take the strain of waiting –
Charlotte: scampering over the blunted causeway
            of Parsonage headstones
Anne: …his stepping stones
Emily: …fire-feet knowing off by heart
All: …each dip and rise and mumbling gap
Emily: …between the leaning graves…

Satanic chapel-goer, fox-haired
disciple of Byron, de Quincy,
opium-puffed, burnt out to cinders
in the clammy squall of needling sweat
clamping his thorny curls to wax brow –
soon he'll gulp his bellyful
from Lethe's dark bowl;
a full tot of broth from the Ferryman's hands
bleached bone-white as his marble skin;
parching soup for insuperable soul.

[*cliffed*: a Cornish expression for 'cast aside' or 'thrown away']

v.

In no time his sisters will follow.

First Emily; her paling dress-rehearsal
at Branwell's chapping funeral
swift as a swallow, stubborn as a thrush,
granite-willed till the end, staggering downstairs
the day she slips with the sprig of heather
from her limp hand on the tattered chaise lounge,
Keeper by her side (the dog she loved
so much she beat him) – crutching her lungs
till the moment she'd known would always come
effortless as the harebells' thrum.
⠀⠀⠀Anne, only a season on, abroad
at Scarborough's sighing sands.
⠀⠀⠀Lastly, Charlotte, spared a tiny life-
time to taste posterity on her tongue...

...the Parson outlasted his progeny,
ringed as a tree, a furniture part,
a hollow-sounding heirloom, now
snowy-plumed as an old barn owl
mummified in his neckerchief...
Goodnight my children – won't stay up too late...

vi.

The raised grave of the Parsonage
stares out the bitter wuthering,
the crooked headstones of the crags,
the darkening brow of tumbled moor.

Four stunted furs battered and bowed
by bashing winds, bark Atlases,
ballast the sky with tensing boughs –
as in seclusion's servitude
their minds, besieged, withstood the storms
and wore them on embattled brows.

A Ghost in the Dark Room

Something seeping in through sepia tones
between yearning faces' desperate belief:
a third face surfaces in the albino
splash of the dark room; a ghostly outline
inking through in the unfocused shadows;
a chink in the chiaroscuro.
Not only a medium's special-filmed eye
discerns this marbling countenance
smudging through like half-wiped chalk
on a blackboard, from the dumb other side.
Ghost photographs number more than bleached
explanations; licked coincidences.
Only the camera's lens shapes the invisible;
only the human eye believes the incredible.

Shadows Die Hard

I was absent for a time while I was young
in all but name accompanied by three
hundred and sixty-five red crosses on
school registers – incarnate absentee.

But I was more than present in my head,
a conscientious, punctual attendee
alive to abstracts, thought forms, realms of gold
that teachers stigmatised as truancy.

Absent I've remained my life so far:
absent at work, though present in body;
absent in body, though present in spirit
with one who always thought me far away;

unreachable; and so stopped reaching me.
But long before, I'd flown the ground to see
words' transforming shadows contour the
unnavigable map of poetry.

In my absence, someone's haunted in my place,
who has a name, a mask, a way, but he
is only partly like me, a vaguer shade
of what I truly am, but cannot be.

He walks the world, he casts a shadow on
the sunlit pavement, but his shadow's me,
while he's some vessel only visible
by the trick of light other people see.

What can I leave behind if I'm not here?
A shadow can't cast shadow. Can I be
absent, and then *more* absent? — I'll bequeath
my absence in absence to posterity.

Hisses from the Palimpsest

i. Introductions

Holistic sanctuary: a plush pause of room
daubed hint-of-lilac – inspiriting change
from the brush-off grey of the counsellor's broom
which can only tidy, drug or rearrange
my thoughts' spilt toy-box. A coin-palmed guide
gifts me gossip from the other side.

ii. Lily and John

First Lily shines through to smile at my urge
to dig up her ceded ideas, ripe
fibres she pitted in napkin serge
for marital trappings' colic tripe;
fears of sheer impulses leaping the edge
to a green repeating end.
                              (The ledge
between tangible and invisible
precarious as our scalloping lobes:
spectres receptive – even visible
in Victorian mediums' mucus robes –
to ghost-Morse tapped by needling clairvoyants
unstitching the distich of existence,
tracing the Braille of the ravelled thread
on table-cloths laced with after-trace;
translating spirits, eavesdropping the dead).

Present, correct, in khaki carapace,
grandfather John, chuffed at my interest
in those I only knew through a palimpsest
of arsclist hiss. No scrape of his smoked tone
this time, just the tight-breathed intermission
of a metacarpal gramophone
cranking sound-waves to crackly transmission
(tracings of passed characters, so they say,
can be taped at a certain time of day).

iii. Beryl and Harold

Next Beryl, my Ugandan-raised grandma –
truncated as her elephant-foot gamp-
stand, yeasty and round, armchair rum baba,
shins like blotched sausages, blimpish with cramp –
vents through to précis on my present spell
of trumped luck: I must toughen up my shell,
pincer on through life's snagging rock-pool
braced in crustacean – apple of her eye
as a halo-haired boy; gold in the buhl
of her tortoiseshell specs.
                                              True as a die,
her under-the-thumb husband Harold,
now demobbed in the other world:
in their lino and woodchip hereafter
I'm told they communicate better
than in stilted life: brake mustard laughter,
since Beryl still seems the tempo-setter,
at least, according to a strained reprise
from the medium's ear-trumpet expertise.

(Psychic? Or bogus reader of vibes?
Pickpocket telepath palming my thoughts?
Or truly inspired in what he transcribes?
He could tap in any time without rapport;
throw me to his circle of thimbled knitters
for their tapestry of absent sitters).

iv. Time's Up

The hour out, his palm clams up. The clock
ticks back: Time's teacherly realigning.
The palimpsest's wiped over on the crock
of coppery chrome – life's tactful self-erasing.
But traces, spectral patinas, remain.
Repeated listens raise them from the grain.

v. Traces

Cassette in hand I drift home with the boon
of ghost companions, an amplified sense
of those passed on but who listen in; spoon
my replication brushed by their absence –
I'm not as out of synch as I often feel
but a variation scratching reel-to-reel.